Happy Birthday!

Birthday Cakes

by Sarah L. Schuette

Consulting editor: Gail Saunders-Smith, PhD

CAPSTONE PRESS
a capstone imprint

Pebble Plus is published by Capstone Press,
151 Good Counsel Drive, P.O. Box 669, Mankato, Minnesota 56002.
www.capstonepress.com

092009
005618CGS10

Books published by Capstone Press are manufactured with paper
containing at least 10 percent post-consumer waste.

Library of Congress Cataloging-in-Publication Data
Schuette, Sarah L., 1976–
   Birthday cakes / by Sarah L. Schuette.
   p. cm. — (Pebble plus. Happy birthday!)
   Includes bibliographical references and index.
   Summary: "Simple text and colorful photographs describe types of birthday cakes" — Provided by publisher.
   ISBN 978-1-4296-3998-9 (library binding)
   1. Cake — Juvenile literature. I. Title. II. Series.
TX771.S29 2010
641.8'653 — dc22   2009026264

Editorial credits
Erika L. Shores, editor; Ashlee Suker, designer; Wanda Winch, media researcher, Eric Manske, production specialist;
   Sarah Schuette, photo stylist; Marcy Morin, scheduler

Photo credits
Capstone Studio/Karon Dubke, all

The Capstone Press Photo Studio thanks Countryside Homes in Mankato, Minnesota, for their help with photo
   shoots for this book.

The author dedicates this book in memory of her Grandma Minnie Simcox who taught her how to bake.

Note to Parents and Teachers

The Happy Birthday! set supports national social studies standards related to culture. This book
describes and illustrates birthday cakes. The images support early readers in understanding
the text. The repetition of words and phrases helps early readers learn new words. This book
also introduces early readers to subject-specific vocabulary words, which are defined in the
Glossary section. Early readers may need assistance to read some words and to use the Table of
Contents, Glossary, Read More, Internet Sites, and Index sections of the book.

Table of Contents

Happy Birthday

Birthday cakes celebrate

your special day.

All kinds of cakes

make sweet birthday treats.

Candles on a birthday cake

tell a person's age.

Maya turns 6 today.

Flavors and Frosting

Cakes are chocolate, white, yellow, or many other flavors. Arthur picks chocolate cake for his party.

9

Frosting, or icing, can be

any color you want.

Pink frosting tastes like

strawberries on Anna's cake.

Fun Cakes

Cakes come in all shapes
and sizes.
A snowman cake celebrates
Lynn's winter birthday.

Cole's cake is shaped

like a race car.

He'll race to finish his piece.

Look at the cupcakes for

Owen's birthday.

Some cupcakes have sprinkles.

Other cupcakes have

round candy pieces.

An ice cream cake tastes cool

on Addie's summer birthday.

Eat it before it melts!

Your Birthday

An ice cream cake?

Cupcakes? A race car?

What kind of cake

do you want this year?

Glossary

candle — a stick of wax with a string or wick that burns to give light

celebrate — to do something fun to mark a special event such as a birthday

cupcake — a small, round cake made in a baking pan that is divided into cups

frosting — a sweet sugar coating used to decorate cakes; frosting is also called icing; it comes in many colors and flavors.

Read More

Blake, Susannah. *Cookies and Cakes.* Make and Eat. New York: PowerKids Press, 2009.

Maurer, Tracy. *Cupcakes, Cookies, and Cakes.* Creative Crafts for Kids. Vero Beach, Fla.: Rourke, 2009.

Powell, Jillian. *A Birthday.* Why Is This Day Special? North Mankato, Minn.: Smart Apple Media, 2007.

Internet Sites

FactHound offers a safe, fun way to find Internet sites related to this book. All of the sites on FactHound have been researched by our staff.

Here's all you do:

Visit *www.facthound.com*

FactHound will fetch the best sites for you!

Index

Word Count: 137
Grade: 1
Early-Intervention Level: 16

24